Financial Achievement Inspired Through Him

A Financial Training Guide to Increasing Your Income & Becoming Debt FREE

Proverbs 9:11-12
11 For through me your days will be many, and years will be added to your life. 12 If you are wise, your wisdom will reward you;

Matthew 25:20-22
20 The man who had received the five talents brought the other five. 'Master,' he said, 'you entrusted me with five talents. See, I have gained five more.' 21 "His master replied, 'Well done, good and faithful servant! You have been faithful with a few things; I will put you in charge of many things.

By
Jimmy Reed
R.E. Investor – Mentor - Trainer

Copyright R.E.E.D. 2008

Read This First

Please allow us to extend our thanks to you for purchasing <u>Financial Achievement Inspired Through Him</u>. It is our sincere hope that this training manual is a blessing to you, your family and your business. We know that when you put the strategies of this course in to practice, you will increase your ability to Increase your Income and lower you expenses.

We also hope that you, in turn, will be a blessing to those who have financial problems. Many of them have no idea what to do with the situation they are in, so they may turn to you to help them solve their problems.

Please take a moment to look inside the manual. **You will find that there are several blanks intentionally left in the material.** <u>You will fill these out during our 1 day workshop or by joining our Network at www.JimmyReed.net</u> ***Once you join the network on our web page you will be sent a confirmation email. Once you confirm that email you will be sent an email with a link at the bottom of the new email. Click the link to go to the <u>Live (recorded) video links</u>. <u>Fill in the blanks as you watch each video segment.</u>***

Finally, please remember that all the material in the manual is copy-written. This information is intended for your eyes only. Please do not make copies of this material, as it would be a violation of copyright law.

As we teach in our Financial Achievement Inspired Through Him Training, keep in mind the heart and idea of serving those less fortunate and doing the right thing all the time. If we all strive to be the best and do what is right, what a difference we could make.

Again, thank you very much for allowing us to show you how to get your finances in order.
We do appreciate your business.

Sincerely,
Jimmy Reed
Real Estate Equity Development, Inc.

Real Estate Equity Development
P.O. Box 122654, Fort Worth, TX. 76121
Office 817-731-0120
www.JimmyReed.net

Copyright R.E.E.D. 2008

Financial Achievement Inspired Through Him

Introduction

Section 1   Our Purpose / Gifts & Talents

Section 2   Economics

Section 3   God's Will For Us *(Read The Scriptures & See How the Spirit Speaks to You)*

Section 4   Personal Financial Statements / Monthly Budgets / Financial Goals

Section 5   Debt Reduction List / Schedule

Section 6   Budget Goals

Section 7   Work

Section 8   Family Influence

Section 9   God, Church, the Marketplace / Tithe & Giving

Section 10   Investing & New or Improved Businesses

Section 11   Putting It All Into Perspective

Section 12   Action Plan

Our Goal with this training is to help folks not to be enslaved to debt anymore. To have us grow closer to God, and to serve Him as He has created us to do so. We also want to increase our giving and tithe to the church. We want to build a stronger unity in families and teach our children to leave an inheritance for their families and generations to come.

This training has been years in the making and we now feel the time has come to put it into action. God wants his children to be in charge of their finances and to be faithful in giving back to Him what he has so lovingly given us. Lastly this book will help me to fulfill my Mission Statement which for years has also been my company's Mission Statement.
Now I want to share it with You!

Copyright R.E.E.D. 2008

Guiding Scripture
Proverbs 3: 1-35

Mission Statement
To provide, and serve those seeking a better way of life the opportunity to invest in their future and to live life full in Gods will. And in return they may go out and share Gods LOVE and help others less fortunate.

Prime Time God Prayer

Dear God, Your Word tells me to cast my cares upon you. Oh how I want to do that, to bring all my cares to you and leave them at your feet. I do not want to be a worrier, but one whose faith is strong to trust you. I want to bring those burdens and concerns to you, and not keep picking them up and worrying about them. May this year be one of spiritual breakthrough in my life and in the lives of those I love. May our lives be filled with joy and peace through your Spirit. May you be the center and the heart of our homes. May we be more Christ like and less like the world in our everyday lives. Help us and have mercy upon us, dear God. Please forgive us of our sins and guide our steps.
In Jesus' name, amen.

We must approach God everyday with the right mind set. We need to seek first the Kingdom of God. We need to know what talents and gifts God has given us. We are designed by God and for God's purpose so we need to know what we are good at and what we like to do.

The best way to start each day will be in Prayer with God. We must also know God and to do that we just need to confess our sins and acknowledge that his son Jesus died on the cross for us so we may have eternal life and a **relationship** with God.

As We start this training remember we must have Faith that God will leads us, provide for us and never leave us. He truly does love us and wants the best for his children. But we must be Faithful.

Copyright R.E.E.D. 2008

Section 1

Our Purpose / Gifts & Talents

What is our purpose here? Most would say to make all the money we can and he who at the end has the most wins! Well sorry to say I do not think that is what God had in mind when he put us here. In fact there are several scriptures that can guide us on our job here on earth such as:

Ecclesiastes 12:13

[13] Now all has been heard;
here is the conclusion of the matter:
Fear God and keep his commandments,
for this is the **whole duty** of man.

Matthew 28: 19-20   The Great Commission

[19] Therefore **go and make disciples** of all nations, baptizing them in the name of the Father and of the Son and of the Holy Spirit, [20] and **teaching them** to obey everything I have commanded you. And surely I am with you always, to the very end of the age."

Luke 10:27

[27] He answered: " **'Love the Lord your God** with all your heart and with all your soul and with all your strength and with all your mind'; and, **'Love your neighbor as yourself.**"

Now most of us may know these from Sunday school and Church service, but do we actually do them? And if we could what would our lives be like? Well we may not have that answer but as we try and define our purpose we need to keep the broad scope of things in perspective. What we need to do now is decide what our purpose is; being that of to serve God and love others and how we put that into <u>action everyday</u> not only in our **personal** lives but in the **work place**.

As we go through this training we are going to learn a lot about how we have been trained and molded to fit into the world and we need to remember we are not of this world.

John 17: 15-18

.[15] My prayer is not that you take them out of the world but that you protect them from the evil one. **[16] They are not of the world, even as I am not of it.** [17] Sanctify them by the truth; your word is truth. [18] As you sent me into the world, I have sent them into the world.

Now how can we serve, fulfill our purpose, and serve God? Let's look at discovering our gifts, what are the talents God has blessed you with? Let's take a moment and below write down what you think may be some of your talents and gifts.

Talents and Gifts

1. _____

2. _____

3. _____

4. _____

5. _____

6. _____

7. _____

Only Seven and for some of you, you may be saying SEVEN! Now these gift and talents may be _____ given or _____ **driven**. We need to determine those that are actually God Given. Are these potential God Gifts things you like to do? Do you do them now? Do they involve family? Are they a part of your Work? And if not can they be incorporated into your life and a way that they **Serve God and Witness to others**?

Let's look at the _____ side of these gifts. We have to work; it's how we make money to pay our bills and put food on the table. God even tells us it is good to work.

Copyright R.E.E.D. 2008

Colossians 3:23

[23] Whatever you do, **work** at it with all your heart, as **working for the Lord**, not for men, [24] since you know that you will receive an **inheritance from the Lord as a reward**. It is the **Lord Christ you are serving**.

Genesis 2:15

[15] The LORD God took the man and put him in the Garden of Eden to **work it and take care of it**. *(The first thing God did is put Adam to work he knew it was good for him)*

Exodus 23:12

[12] "Six days **do your work**, but on the seventh day **do not work**,"
(He also knew it was good for us to rest he did it himself)

Proverbs 12:14

[14] From the fruit of his lips a man is filled with good things as surely as the **work of his hands rewards him**.
(We are paid or compensated for the work we do)

Ephesians 2:10

[10] For we are **God's work**manship, created in Christ Jesus **to do good works**, which God prepared in advance for us to do. *(We are created to do these works of service)*

** Ecclesiastes 4:9**

[9] Two are better than one, because they have a **good return for their work**
(And as couples in marriage or business partners we have a better return for our work)

So we need to work for many reasons but most of all it is pleasing to God. It is God's way of providing for us and we are paid for the type of work we do. Based on the type of talents & gifts we have, determines the jobs we have which also determines how much we can be paid.

Copyright R.E.E.D. 2008

Section 2

Economics

In *section 1* we determined our gifts and talents and learned that God wants us to work, and it is work that we now take a look at to see where we are in our lives with <u>WORK</u>!

Is work all we do all the time? Or do we hardly work at all? I can tell you from experience you need a balance of the two.

We also need to get familiar with Economics and how it effect's our lives, our world, and work. We have the old standard and my favorite phrase *"Supply and Demand"* Basic economics 101. Don't worry we are not going to bore you with a semester of economics, just some basics and how it applies to our goal in this training.

Let's start with the _____ where business is done. In the early church there was really no separation between work and church. In fact many of Jesus followers remained in their jobs while still ministering. They used there jobs to help minister to others. Today however we have a different worldly view of this. We have separated in most cases work from church. We need to keep this in the fore front of our minds that the work place should honor God. We should not be trying to keep him out of the workplace but make Him the focus of it.

As we talk about supply and demand we need to first know what is our passion in life and what gifts has God given us? Once we know this we need to know how we use these gifts and passions to create a business and or do the work we were designed for.

What does the market place feel about the business we want to create or already have?

Is there a _____ for the _____ we provide?

Will this demand provide the _____ we are looking for?

And can we supply the time, skills, and energy to provide the service?

Example my business is real estate, but there are several levels to my business which will be discussed later. However it does fill a need, people need a place to live so in real estate there is a huge demand for shelter. It is a necessity which makes it more desirable by the consumer. If you had a business in the food industry that would be a very strong demand type business.

So let's recap what we know so far.

We need to supply a service or product that has a high demand.

At the same time honoring God with how and where we do our business.

Remember everything we have is truly God's and he has in trusted us to be good honorable stewards over it all.

Now let's look further into economics once we find that desire of what we want to do how do we implement it? How to start a business? How to better the one we are already in?

Wow that is a whole other training right there.

So let's sum it up with this, some businesses require training, just as many investors I have taught over the years came to me for training on how to be a Real Estate Investor. You may need some training to be able to start the business you desire or additional training to become better at the job you currently have.

So as we move forward we will also need a_____, a step by step procedure of what we need to do to be able to provide the service to our consumer.

On the next page let's fill out a fact sheet.

Fact Sheet

What type of business are we interested in?
_____

Do we already know about this business and or have experience in it?
_____

If not do we need more training? _____ If so what kind?
_____

Do we currently have a step by step **plan** of how to get this business up and going, or how to take it to the next level? (*Now think about this before answering*)
_____

Do we know of other people in this business that could help us, give us advice, and tell us how they did it, sort of a **Mentor** to us on how to do it?
_____

Do you think this could be what God has **designed you** to do?
_____

Would this business make enough money to **provide** for you and your family?
_____

List the **skills & talents** you currently have that would help you in this business.

1. _____

2. _____

3. _____

4. _____

5. _____

6. _____

7. _____

Copyright R.E.E.D. 2008

Did you have seven, or less than seven? If less than seven are you sure this is the business for you? The skills you have are from God. Maybe you have a few skills and the passion to do it but maybe you need some extra training to help you get there. Remember scripture can guide us on many of our choices.

Hosea 4:6

6 my people are destroyed from **lack of knowledge**.

Isaiah 56:10

10 Israel's watchmen are blind, **they all lack knowledge;**

Remember we must do all our work unto the Lord and do it well, so training is necessary in the work place. We have all had jobs in the past and we were trained for those jobs. We went to school to learn different skills so we would be prepared for the market place. Now keep in mind our education system, in my opinion, it trains us to get jobs not necessarily to be _____.

What is an Entrepreneur? And are you one? This is hard to say I feel it is a desire in you that wants to make us go higher up in life. To be more than what we thought we could ever be. To achieve something our parents and grandparents did not. Maybe it's to be leaders, or visionaries, not to be just complacent.

Now I am not talking about contentment. We should be content as scripture tell us to. But to be what I have called for years a "_____".

To me the top elite mind setters, entrepreneurs, geniuses; what ever you want to call them I have for years called them the 3 Percenters. They are truly the _____ of the world.

And I feel we must always have **that** _____ **set** to be able to achieve the highest goals we may have set for ourselves in life.

Now let's talk about problem solving, we are always going to have problems in business. We must be able to handle them with strength and Faith. How we respond to problems can be a witness to others who see us. So we do not want to react as I like to say hysterical but instead with composure. Look at the problem, analyze it for what it is, and then determine can I solve it? If you cannot solve it who can?

Copyright R.E.E.D. 2008

Remember in business we must have a _____ of experts to help us succeed. In fact this is one of my favorite scriptures.

Proverbs 12:15

15 The way of a fool seems right to him,
    but a **wise man listens to advice**.

Now let's do a final recap of Sections 1 & 2

First recap was

Find out what we are good at and what _____ & _____ we have.

Does our work / business fit into _____ purpose?

We need to supply a _____ or product that has a high _____.

At the same time _____ God with how and where we do our business.

Remember everything we have is truly Gods and he has _____ us to be good honorable stewards over it all.

Second recap

Let's get the _____ (Filled out Fact sheet), need to have this done.

Let's get the training we need to succeed.

And decide that we are, and always will be _____ _____.

And we will put a _____ together to give us counsel in our business.

Copyright R.E.E.D. 2008

God's Will For Us
(Remember to Read the Scriptures & See How the Spirit Speaks to You)

God's Will
How do we know it? Or even get it!

First we must realize to get, or to know Gods will we must have **Faith**. Our Faith comes from believing in **God**, and in **Jesus Christ**. That we believe, and accept, that Christ died on the cross for our sins and was resurrected to eternal life, and in believing and accepting that, we are saved by God's grace (Ephesians 2:8). God loved us so much that he gave us His Grace and His only Son so we may have life and live. He also gave us His **Holy Spirit**, so in living our lives, we could be led to serve Him, and to do His will.

1. We must have **Faith!**
     John 20: 24-31 *read*
             20:29 Blessed are those who have not seen and yet have believed
     Hebrews 11: 1-6 *read*
             11:6 Without Faith we cannot please God

2. If we have Faith, how do we **live for God**?
     1 Peter 4: 1-11 *read*
             4:2 Will of God
             4:8 Above all love
             4:11 Speak the words of God & Let all Glory and praise go to him

3. The will of God - **Trust and Obey God**
     Ephesians 5: 15- 21 *read*
             5:17 Understand the Lords Will

     Micah 6: 8 *read*
             6:8 Walk with God

4. **What is His will for me? And how do I know?**
     Romans 12: 1-2 *read*
             12:1 Living sacrifices
             12:2 Be Transformed

Copyright R.E.E.D. 2008

Test and approve what God's Will is

Romans 12: 3-21 *read*

How do I know if it's Gods Will? _____ **And here's how.**
    1. Is it _____.
    2. Do I have _____.
    3. Are the _____.

1. **Example:** _____ I see something I want, do I take it? **No,** the bible tells us not to steal. But what about in a different situation, **using the famous,** all my friends are doing _____ (*you fill in the blank*), and I don't see in the bible where it says I specifically cannot do it. So is it ok to do it?

   What do we do? _____
   What if we don't get an answer? _____
   What if we don't like the answer? _____
   _____

2. **Example:** _____ I feel it is from God, and it does not go against biblical principal. And I can sleep well at night, and I don't continually agonize about it, it's just not a burden. But most of us seem to get this situation, I think its God's will but I am just not sure if I am at peace with it, I'm somewhat confused.

   So now what do I do?
   Continue to Pray and ask God to _____ his will to you.
   Remember if you are <u>confused</u>, it is not from God. *The devil is always trying to confuse us. We need to continually pray and keep strong in Gods word.*
   <u>**Remember God will give you 1 of 3 answers,**</u>
       1. _____
       2. _____
       3. _____
   Sometimes we <u>don't</u> get an answer, because God is not ready for us to know His will in a particular circumstance until the time is right.
   So we should be _____! *I know we don't like this however it can be the testing of our perseverance, and faith.*
   But now I do have peace, and it seems to be in line with the bible, what do I do? _____

Copyright R.E.E.D. 2008

3. **Example:** _____ The doors seem to be opening, or closing, I have peace about it, and it does not seem to go against scripture. What do I do?

First the Hard Question. <u>Is God opening the doors, or is it Satan?</u>

This is where our questions and answers become difficult ones. We don't always know a **100%**. But if we have tested it, have peace about it, and it seems the door is open, even though we know Satan could be opening it. What do we do?

    1. Keep our _____ on God. Pray, Listen, and Obey!
    2. _____ Him in **all things** and he will make your paths straight.
    Read Proverbs 3:6, Psalms 32:8, Isaiah 42:16

So now we have a choice, do we go forward and allow our **<u>Faith</u>** in God to lead us? Or do we sit back and continue to wait? Each of us will respond differently. If we move forward, and it does not turn out the way we want it to, did we not follow God's will?

Or if we choose to do nothing, is that a lack of **Faith** (*James 1:5-6*)? God wants us to all prosper and ask for all he has in store for us. We just need to be faithful and praying, and asking Him for it. Make sure our motives are always those that will honor God and please Him (*Romans 8:26-27*). Put God in the center of our lives, not ourselves (*John 15:5*).

Remember what Jesus said: *I will always be with you.*   *(Read Matthew 28:19-20)*

He promises never to leave us, if we make wrong choices, God will use them for his better purpose (*Romans 8:28*). If we walk through a door, and it's slammed in our face, seek God and move to the next door. He loves to see our Faith in action. Seek him First and all will be given.

Including His will for your life.

Isaiah 43:2-4

2 When you pass through the waters, I will be with you; and when you pass through the rivers, they will not sweep over you. When you walk through the fire, you will not be burned; the flames will not set you ablaze. 3 For I am the LORD, your God, the Holy One of Israel, your Savior; I give Egypt for your ransom, Cush and Seba in your stead. 4 Since you are precious and honored in my sight, and because I love you, I will give men in exchange for you, and people in exchange for your life.

Copyright R.E.E.D. 2008

Section 4

Personal Financial Statements / Monthly Budgets / Financial Goals

Now let's get down and dirty and make this stuff work. Time to gather financial **Junk**!
We need to assess what we have coming in and out of our household. We need to be able to track our **Income and Expenses.**

So we need to fill out several work sheets *(for class fill out estimates, then use the extra copy to go in detail over the next couple of days at home.)*

First up is our _____
We will use this to see what we have in assets already, along with our liabilities. And determine our net worth.

Second will be our _____
We will use this to track our Income, Tithe/Giving, Taxes, Housing, Food, Auto, Gas, etc...

Third we are going to set up _____
This will help us set goals for tithing, Debt Reduction Payments, and Savings Goals.

And Last _____(Section5)
This will be used as a plan to pay off our debt and become Debt Free!

Now keep in mind this is all for our personal side of our finances, you will need to do the same for your business side if you are self employed or have some kind of business set up for extra income. By the way we will talk more about this later. It is something we all need to have to help us reduce debt faster and increase our savings.

Now on these sheets we have provided keep in mind they are what I call "Old School". I personally did not use these because I have used a computer software program to do it for me since about 1999. I like the computer programs much better, and they are much more detailed and easier to pull up reports and graphs. Basically they are way smarter than me and definitely much faster.

All Right take a deep breath and say

"It's Gonna Be Alllllll Right!"

Ok let's Fill them Out!

Copyright R.E.E.D. 2008

Personal Financial Statement
(For Class Use)

Assets (*Current Value*)

Cash in Accounts	$_____
Savings	$_____
Stock, CD & Bonds	$_____
Cash Value of Insurance	$_____
Coins, Gold, Jewelry, Art etc…	$_____
Home	$_____
Other Real Estate	$_____
Notes (Mortgages) Receivable	$_____
Automobiles, Motorcycles, Boats	$_____
Furniture	$_____
Other Personal Property	$_____
Pension / Retirement	$_____
Other Assets	$_____

Total Assets $_____

Liabilities (*Current Amount Owed*)

Credit Cards	$_____
Home Mortgage	$_____
Other Real Estate Loans	$_____
Automobile Loans	$_____
Personal Debt / Loans to Friends	$_____
School Loans	$_____
Medical Bills	$_____
Life Insurance Loans	$_____
Bank Loans (Include CD, Stock)	$_____
Entertainment Loans TV, Stereo,	$_____
Other Debt / Loans	$_____

Total Liabilities $_____

Net Worth (Total Assets minus Total Liabilities) $_____

Copyright R.E.E.D. 2008

Personal Financial Statement
(For Home Detailed Use)

Assets (*Current Value*)
- Cash in Accounts $_____
- Savings $_____
- Stock, CD & Bonds $_____
- Cash Value of Insurance $_____
- Coins, Gold, Jewelry, Art etc… $_____
- Home $_____
- Other Real Estate $_____
- Notes (Mortgages) Receivable $_____
- Automobiles, Motorcycles, Boats $_____
- Furniture $_____
- Other Personal Property $_____
- Pension / Retirement $_____
- Other Assets $_____

Total Assets $_____

Liabilities (*Current Amount Owed*)
- **Credit Cards** $_____
- **Home Mortgage** $_____
- **Other Real Estate Loans** $_____
- **Automobile Loans** $_____
- **Personal Debt / Loans to Friends** $_____
- **School Loans** $_____
- **Medical Bills** $_____
- **Life Insurance Loans** $_____
- **Bank Loans** (Include CD, Stock) $_____
- **Entertainment Loans TV, Stereo,** $_____
- **Other Debt / Loans** $_____

Total Liabilities $_____

Net Worth (Total Assets minus Total Liabilities) $_____

Copyright R.E.E.D. 2008

Monthly Budget
(For Class Use)

Income

Work	$	
2nd Business	$	
Rental, Dividends, Retirement	$	
Any Other Income	$	

Total Income $_____

Expenses

Tithe / Giving	$	
Taxes	$	
Housing / Mortgage	$	
Food	$	
Automobile Payments	$	
Gas / Maintenance	$	
Insurance	$	
Credit Cards	$	
Credit Cards	$	
Credit Cards	$	
Credit Cards	$	
Credit Cards	$	
Clothing	$	
Entertainment (Cable, Internet, etc.)	$	
Medical	$	
Savings	$	
Investments	$	
School / Daycare	$	
Miscellaneous Expenses	$	

Total Expenses $_____

Net Result (Take Total Income minus Total Expenses = Surplus/ Deficit) $_____

Copyright R.E.E.D. 2008

Monthly Budget
(For Home Detailed Use)

Income

Work	$_____
2nd Business	$_____
Rental, Dividends, Retirement	$_____
Any Other Income	$_____

Total Income $_____

Expenses

Tithe / Giving	$_____
Taxes	$_____
Housing / Mortgage	$_____
Food	$_____
Automobile Payments	$_____
Gas / Maintenance	$_____
Insurance	$_____
Credit Cards	$_____
Credit Cards	$_____
Credit Cards	$_____
Credit Cards	$_____
Credit Cards	$_____
Clothing	$_____
Entertainment (Cable, Internet, etc.)	$_____
Medical	$_____
Savings	$_____
Investments	$_____
School / Daycare	$_____
Miscellaneous Expenses	$_____

Total Expenses $_____

Net Result (Take Total Income minus Total Expenses = Surplus/ Deficit) $_____

Copyright R.E.E.D. 2008

Financial Goals
*(Use at Home and **Pray** About It)*

Date __/__/____ for Goals to Start.

Giving Goals

 <u>Tithe / Giving</u> Out of the First of Each Check of INCOME _____% of that Income.

 Other Giving & Support Goals: _____
_____
_____

Debt Repayment Goals
 I would like to pay off the following debt first.

Creditor (Credit Cards, Auto, School etc…)	Amount (Balance)
_____	$_____
_____	$_____
_____	$_____
_____	$_____
_____	$_____
_____	$_____

Investment Goals *(These can help reduce our debt & Increase our Income)*
 I will put back each month _____% of MY INCOME into a

Investment   Total Amount Needed
(CD, Money Market, IRA, Down Payment on <u>Rental Property</u> etc.)

Investment	Total Amount Needed
_____	$_____
_____	$_____
_____	$_____

Education Goals
 I would like to Fund the Following Education

Person	School	Annual Cost	Total Cost
_____	_____	$_____	$_____
_____	_____	$_____	$_____
_____	_____	$_____	$_____
_____	_____	$_____	$_____

Page 1 of Financial Goals

Copyright R.E.E.D. 2008

Savings Goal
     I Would Like to Put Back ____% of MY INCOME each Month.

Type of Savings (Savings Account, CD, Mutual Fund etc…)
_____
_____

Starting a Business?
I would like to Invest In My/Our business   Yes____   No____   If NO Why? _____

Type of Business
_____

What Skills Do I Have? *(Remember Talent and Gifts and the Fact Sheet)*
_____
_____

What Skills or Training Will I Need?
_____
_____

Will the Supply and Demand Still be Right at the time I Start?
_____

Could This Business Reduce My Debt Faster and Increase My Savings?
_____

What Standard of Living Do I have Now? And What Standard do I desire? And does it please the Lord? *(Take a moment and prayerfully consider before answering)*
_____
_____
_____
_____
_____
_____

Page 2 of Financial Goals

Copyright R.E.E.D. 2008

Section 5

Debt Reduction List / Schedule

Now let's tackle the toughest of our problems Debt Reduction. We have no problem creating it, but to get rid of it that is another story. Anyway we need to become debt free scripture says:

Deuteronomy 28:12

12 "-You will lend to many nations but **will borrow from none**."

I really like This One

Proverbs 22:7

Just as the rich rule the poor, so **the borrower is servant to the lender**... (NLT Ver.)

Ok let's use the Debt Repayment Schedule to help us eliminate our Debt.

We need to 1st _____.

The Monthly Payments.

Balance Due.

Interest Rates.

Payments Past Due.

<u>And What Did We BUY?</u> *(Food on credit cards not good unless paid off each month in full)*

Next we need to set up a schedule to pay back and pay off our debt.

We need the date the bill is due.

Copyright R.E.E.D. 2008

Payment Amount.

Payments remaining.

And the Balance Remaining after each payment is made.

We are going to break the list into 4 sections

Creditors *(Credit Card Companies such as VISA, Master Card, Sears, Best Buy etc…)*

Then Auto Loans *(Cars, Motorcycles, Boats, ATV's, Wave Runners all those Toys)*

Then the BIG ONE the Home Mortgage *(If you Rent really consider buying)*

Then any Business / Investment Debt *(This one has several variations for me)*

I think a lot of business debt can be good debt. My goal is to get you personally debt free. And the right business debt can help you achieve that. Some may disagree but I am only showing you how I did it.

So the next form is ready for us to tackle. You will do this in more detail at home but we are going to discuss it here today to understand why it is so important to set this list up and have a disciplined attitude on making it actually work.

You will need to make some _____ to reaching your goals. To become debt free will take a lot of effort on your part. However the rewards are incredible. When you are debt free you actually have less:

Stress – *You can live longer and healthier.*

Have more time to enjoy life, family, and friends.

And most of all you can actually Serve God more; *remember that is what we are here for to serve.*

By the way let me say it now before I forget, always go back and _____ this manual, it can help you get ____ _____ as you read a lot of the scriptures that will help you accomplish your goals and God's will for you.

Ok Let's do it, Fill out the Debt Reduction List & Schedule Form.

Copyright R.E.E.D. 2008

Debt Reduction List *(For Class Use)*

Date __/__/____ *(For Reductions to Start)*

Creditor	What was Purchased	Monthly Payments	Balance Due	Interest Rate	Scheduled Pay off Date	Payments Past Due
_____	_____	$_____	$_____	_____%	__/__/____	#_____
_____	_____	$_____	$_____	_____%	__/__/____	#_____
_____	_____	$_____	$_____	_____%	__/__/____	#_____
_____	_____	$_____	$_____	_____%	__/__/____	#_____
_____	_____	$_____	$_____	_____%	__/__/____	#_____
_____	_____	$_____	$_____	_____%	__/__/____	#_____
_____	_____	$_____	$_____	_____%	__/__/____	#_____
_____	_____	$_____	$_____	_____%	__/__/____	#_____
Totals Creditor		$_____	$_____			

Auto Loans

_____		$_____	$_____	_____%	__/__/____	#_____
_____		$_____	$_____	_____%	__/__/____	#_____
Totals Auto		$_____	$_____			

Home Mortgage

_____		$_____	$_____	_____%	__/__/____	#_____
Totals Mortgage		$_____	$_____			

Business / Investment Debt

_____		$_____	$_____	_____%	__/__/____	#_____
_____		$_____	$_____	_____%	__/__/____	#_____
Totals Business / Investment		$_____	$_____			

Copyright R.E.E.D. 2008

Debt Reduction List *(Home Detailed Use)*

Date __/__/____ *(For Reductions to Start)*

Creditor	What was Purchased	Monthly Payments	Balance Due	Interest Rate	Scheduled Pay off Date	Payments Past Due
_____	_____	$_____	$_____	_____%	__/__/____	#_____
_____	_____	$_____	$_____	_____%	__/__/____	#_____
_____	_____	$_____	$_____	_____%	__/__/____	#_____
_____	_____	$_____	$_____	_____%	__/__/____	#_____
_____	_____	$_____	$_____	_____%	__/__/____	#_____
_____	_____	$_____	$_____	_____%	__/__/____	#_____
_____	_____	$_____	$_____	_____%	__/__/____	#_____
_____	_____	$_____	$_____	_____%	__/__/____	#_____
Totals Creditor		$_____	$_____			

Auto Loans

_____		$_____	$_____	_____%	__/__/____	#_____
_____		$_____	$_____	_____%	__/__/____	#_____
Totals Auto		$_____	$_____			

Home Mortgage

_____		$_____	$_____	_____%	__/__/____	#_____
Totals Mortgage		$_____	$_____			

Business / Investment Debt

_____		$_____	$_____	_____%	__/__/____	#_____
_____		$_____	$_____	_____%	__/__/____	#_____
Totals Business / Investment		$_____	$_____			

Copyright R.E.E.D. 2008

Debt Reduction Schedule *(Home Use, After Prayerful Consideration)*

Date __/__/____ *(Start Date)*

Creditor:	What Was Purchased	Balance Owed	Interest
_____	_____	_____	_____

Due Date	$Amount	Payments Remaining	Balance Due
_____	_____	_____	_____
_____	_____	_____	_____
_____	_____	_____	_____
_____	_____	_____	_____
_____	_____	_____	_____
_____	_____	_____	_____
_____	_____	_____	_____
_____	_____	_____	_____
_____	_____	_____	_____
_____	_____	_____	_____
_____	_____	_____	_____
_____	_____	_____	_____
_____	_____	_____	_____
_____	_____	_____	_____
_____	_____	_____	_____

Copyright R.E.E.D. 2008

Debt Re Payment Schedule *(Home Use, After Prayerful Consideration)*

Date __/__/_____ *(Start Date)*

Creditor: What Was Purchased   Balance Owed   Interest

_____   _____   _____   _____

Due Date $Amount   Payments Remaining   Balance Due

_____   _____   _____   _____

_____   _____   _____   _____

_____   _____   _____   _____

_____   _____   _____   _____

_____   _____   _____   _____

_____   _____   _____   _____

_____   _____   _____   _____

_____   _____   _____   _____

_____   _____   _____   _____

_____   _____   _____   _____

_____   _____   _____   _____

_____   _____   _____   _____

_____   _____   _____   _____

_____   _____   _____   _____

Copyright R.E.E.D. 2008

Debt Re Payment Schedule *(Home Use, After Prayerful Consideration)*

Date __/__/____ *(Start Date)*

Creditor: What Was Purchased   Balance Owed   Interest

_____   _____   _____   _____

Due Date $Amount   Payments Remaining   Balance Due

_____   _____   _____   _____
_____   _____   _____   _____
_____   _____   _____   _____
_____   _____   _____   _____
_____   _____   _____   _____
_____   _____   _____   _____
_____   _____   _____   _____
_____   _____   _____   _____
_____   _____   _____   _____
_____   _____   _____   _____
_____   _____   _____   _____
_____   _____   _____   _____
_____   _____   _____   _____
_____   _____   _____   _____
_____   _____   _____   _____

Copyright R.E.E.D. 2008

What is the biggest problem with Debt? _____!

Look at the samples below of how interest can ruin you.

House Purchased for	$100,000.00	
Your monthly mortgage Payment is	$877.57	
Months Paid	X 360	
Total Payments	$315,925.20	$215,925.20 **GONE!**

Say you have Credit Card Debt Balance	$5,560.00
@ 18% interest	
Cost a year in Interest	$1,000.00

Amount of Interest you paid:

Year 5	Year 10	Year 20
$5,000	$10,000	$20,000

Here is what you could have earned on the $1,000 invested at 12%

Year 5	Year 10	Year 20
$6,353	17,549	$72,052

Here is what the Lender earns from your payment at 18%

Year 5	Year 10	Year 20
$7,154	23,521	$146,628

Copyright R.E.E.D. 2008

Debt, Debt, Debt!

Let's start with a warning from God

Proverbs 22:7

7 The rich rule over the poor,
   and the **borrower is servant to the lender**.

This is the one that did it for me.

Now lets look how Americans deal with it.

National Debt: Check out this site **www._____.com** click on National Debt. This is a running clock on our national debt as it goes up, and has other statistics such as Social Security and other things that might need your attention.

As of this month the amount is **$_____** Dollars. When you divide that among approximately _____ people in the USA it means your part is about **$_____**

Now make that check out to….. Oh sorry we can just let it slide.

Folks this is about 1.57 billion a day that the debt keeps going up.

How about Credit Card Debt!

Personal Debt: Check out **www._____.com** this site has a lot of shocking information.

Such as Consumer Revolving Debt, that's us, and as of 2007 it was $904 Billion dollars. I also learned there are over 450 million credit cards in this country. Remember how many live here?

Let's look at scripture.

Deuteronomy 28:12

12 The LORD will open the heavens, the storehouse of his bounty, to send rain on your land in season and to bless all the work of your hands. **You will lend to many nations but will borrow from none.**

WE Have to Get Out of DEBT!!!

Copyright R.E.E.D. 2008

Let look at Business Debt, now this can get a little controversial. There are sites that show Corporate America is driving up the debt also. Executives just doing what ever it takes to fill there pockets regardless of the economy, morals, or the workers. Remember Enron?

Now I struggled as I did my first Stewardship training when it came to business debt. I didn't have a problem being debt free on the personal side but I made my living leveraging real estate.

I sought counsel from some of the leaders in that national organization and realized that if structured right and in a way where I was not personally liable that it would be all right.

I could buy rental property or any real estate; get a loan on it, as long as the property was the collateral for the debt. In my business it is known as a non recourse note. I could leverage the lenders money to buy the property, and from that Cash Flow make the debt payment and keep the difference of the Income minus all the expenses as **my _____Cash Flow**.

Now we will talk later about this!

Some of you though might be asking how I find that lender. EASY!

LOOK!

Oh Yeah and ASK! *Go home and read* **James 4:2**

Well the main thing here for me is:

1. Stop adding to your Personal Debt
2. You need to pray about creating Business Debt. And only if you are not liable for it personally.

Let's look at scripture

Proverbs 22:26-27

26 Do not be a man who strikes hands in pledge or puts up security for debts;
27 if you lack the means to pay, your very bed will be snatched from under you.

In Closing on the issue of DEBT. We need to get out of it. It is not good for us or our country.

As far as **Business Debt** I am good with it.

You need to seek God on your decision with it.

Copyright R.E.E.D. 2008

Section 6

Budget Goals

Now we have to start the dreaded Budget. This may be the hardest thing I had to overcome. To actually have to follow a set amount of spending each month. To try with all the power you can to not go shopping, or avoid: *"look honey a Garage Sale"* That by the way is nearly impossible.

But don't lose heart it can be done!

The key is you and your spouse need to look your budget over often, at least once every week.

When you do need to go shopping make sure you **both pray** before you go. And if you happen to see something you think you need, don't just buy it _____! Go home and pray about it, is the **Holy Spirit** leading you to buy it? Is it necessary? A lot of times if you wait to buy and think and pray about it, you will find that a _____ may have been just a _____. And after a little time that impulse to have it is gone.

A lot of marketing out there is designed to push those buttons inside you that make you react it's why they call it _____ buying.

Now the budget on the next page will take some time to fill out. Many may think it looks a lot like the **Monthly Budget** we did earlier. And it sort of is except it's more **detailed** and it's going to be **a goal for us to establish a NEW** Budget so were not **enslaved** by the one we currently have.

This will help us to reduce what's been going out and to increase what is coming in. And to use what is coming in better than we have been before. We also want to keep in mind this new budget is to be using what God has given us better than we have in the past, and to help us get to where we can spend more time serving God.

Keep in mind God is about relationships. He wants you to spend a lot of time with him: in prayer, His word, and just plain quiet time with Him.

And if you are always rushing out to get to work to make money to pay off all that debt, then your focus is most likely not on God as much as it should be.

So now take a little time in prayer with your spouse and discuss how to estimate your new budget.

Oh one last thing I want to encourage you to do if you are married. And that is to each day spend time together in prayer. You can't imagine how it can change your day and your relationship with your spouse. By the way it pleases God.

Copyright R.E.E.D. 2008

Budget Goals Sheet

Monthly Income

Gross Monthly Income	$ _____	
Salary	$ _____	
Interest	$ _____	
Dividends	$ _____	
Other Income	$ _____	
Less Tithe / Giving	$ _____	
Less Taxes	$ _____	

Net Spendable Income $ _____

Monthly Expenses

Housing $ _____
- Mortgage / Rent $ _____
- Property Taxes $ _____
- Insurance $ _____
- Electric $ _____
- Gas $ _____
- Water $ _____
- Trash $ _____
- Phone $ _____
- Cable / Internet $ _____
- Repairs $ _____
- Other $ _____

Food $ _____
- Groceries $ _____
- Eating Out $ _____
- Misc. $ _____

Transportation $ _____
- Auto Payments $ _____
- Gas / Oil $ _____
- Insurance $ _____
- Licenses / Taxes $ _____
- Repairs $ _____
- Other $ _____

Insurance $ _____
- Life $ _____
- Health $ _____
- Other $ _____

Debt List $ _____

Entertainment $ _____
- Vacation $ _____
- Pets $ _____
- Dates / Sitters $ _____
- Movies $ _____
- Other $ _____

Clothing $ _____

Medical $ _____
- Doctor $ _____
- Dentist $ _____
- Prescriptions $ _____
- Other $ _____

Household Supplies $ _____
- Laundry $ _____
- Cleaning sup. $ _____
- Cosmetics $ _____
- Hair / Barber $ _____
- Necessities $ _____
- Gifts $ _____
- Other $ _____

Child Care $ _____
School $ _____
Investments $ _____

Total Expenses $ _____

Net Spendable Income $ _____
Less Monthly Expenses $ _____
Surplus or Deficit $ _____

Copyright R.E.E.D. 2008

Budget Goals Sheet *(Extra Copy)*

Monthly Income

Gross Monthly Income	$_____	
Salary	$_____	
Interest	$_____	
Dividends	$_____	
Other Income	$_____	
Less Tithe / Giving		$_____
Less Taxes		$_____

Net Spendable Income $_____

Monthly Expenses

Housing	$_____
Mortgage / Rent	$_____
Property Taxes	$_____
Insurance	$_____
Electric	$_____
Gas	$_____
Water	$_____
Trash	$_____
Phone	$_____
Cable / Internet	$_____
Repairs	$_____
Other	$_____

Food	$_____
Groceries	$_____
Eating Out	$_____
Misc.	$_____

Transportation	$_____
Auto Payments	$_____
Gas / Oil	$_____
Insurance	$_____
Licenses / Taxes	$_____
Repairs	$_____
Other	$_____

Insurance	$_____
Life	$_____
Health	$_____
Other	$_____

Debt List	$_____

Entertainment	$_____
Vacation	$_____
Pets	$_____
Dates / Sitters	$_____
Movies	$_____
Other	$_____

Clothing	$_____

Medical	$_____
Doctor	$_____
Dentist	$_____
Prescriptions	$_____
Other	$_____

Household Supplies	$_____
Laundry	$_____
Cleaning sup.	$_____
Cosmetics	$_____
Hair / Barber	$_____
Necessities	$_____
Gifts	$_____
Other	$_____

Child Care	$_____
School	$_____
Investments	$_____

Total Expenses $_____

Net Spendable Income $_____
Less Monthly Expenses $_____
Surplus or Deficit $_____

Copyright R.E.E.D. 2008

Section 7

Work

Back to WORK!

Again we are talking about work. We touched on it some in section 1. We had some scripture that told us work is good and God wants us to work for many reasons. But let's talk about work now in the idea of what we have gone over in Sections 4 – 6. It will take a lot of work just to get these budgets, expenses, and goal sheets just filled out. So think back about being a **3 Percenter**. That's right, are we going to rise to the occasion? Or will we say "Ok I'm fine where I am" Only you can make that decision.

EASY!

EASY!

EASSSSY!

I have my students say this all the time to **train their mind to believe it**. I believe that if I say it enough it will be **Easy**. I see a lot of students get frustrated when I ask them to do this every time I do it over a 3 day training class. I hate to see it because I know they have already given up. They have told themselves it won't work, this is ridiculous, and I didn't pay all this money to say Easy all day long.

Understand one of the most influential books I have ever read was **Think and Grow Rich**. What does that title say? What stands out to you? For most it's the word Rich. For me it was **Think!** I actually never finished the book; it pumped me up so much my mind was saying get going. I didn't know then that I was apparently a 3 Percenter. I just knew it would work if I would _____. It told me it would! And **I BELIEVED!**

Do you _____?
Can you see yourself in 5 years maybe 10, and having your Debt removed and your Income Increased?
Do you believe you can make it happen?

Did you know all you have to do is Work Hard, and the Lord can Reward you for your work.

Well now we need a step by step _____!
Let's discuss what kind of plan we need so we can get to work.

Copyright R.E.E.D. 2008

A Plan or a Goal needs to be written out clearly with what we need to do to reach certain targets or goals we have set.

It needs to be what I call _____ **Goals**. Something that can be obtainable in less than 30 days. Why 30 days _____ **goals** in the beginning help us feel we are moving forward, that's important when you are trying something new. Most folks quit if they do not see that they have made progress within about 6 -8 weeks. We call them **97 Percenters**.

Our goals need to be the _____ stuff at first, then checked off our **"to do"** list. As we progress we will have some 3 month, 6 month, and 1 year goals. Do not make the mistake I did when I started out. I made 1 big goal of 13 million Dollars. Stuck it on a sticky note and stuck it up on the bathroom mirror. By the way I had no deadline to it no steps on how to do it. Just a big ol goal of 13 million DOLLARS!

I found out 9 months later I actually had to **do some** _____ to start moving in the direction of obtaining that goal. I also had to break it down to how many years to get it. Then break that down to how much a month I would have to make. Then I had to break it down to how much a week and finally how much a day. **And that's all it took,** to figure out I needed to change my goal; there was no way I could make that much money a day. My mind was now in **Think and Grow POOR! Mode.**

Thank God I learned about **creating** _____ over time and not necessarily having to have 13 million in cold cash. But instead having something more obtainable which was a _____! I really didn't need 13 million cash I just need to have income and some sort of vehicle that could work harder than me and make that Net Worth go up in value. This is why we filled out the **Personal Financial Statement.** We want to create Income for us now, and in the future by Investing in things that can do that for us. It's known as working _____ not _____. Nothing wrong with hard work but I would rather work Smart!

Will talk later about investing, but now let's get back to working!

We will most likely in the beginning have to put in some extra hours, on top of our normal hours. But do not give up your time with God; that is the most important thing in our lives. Trust me I have had weeks even months where I spent less time with God and more time on MY Goals. Let me tell you now it just does not work. Usually you end up with frustration, stress, and just plain wore out. God wants us to **wait on Him he will lead us in His TIME!**

He also wants us to **remember** _____! **WE need it, and it's biblical.** And then he wants us to spend time with our **families**. Please do not forget this!

Copyright R.E.E.D. 2008

Let's recap Work

1. Work is Good.
2. We have scripture that tell us it is good. *(Read Them)*
3. We want to be a 3%.
4. We need to tell ourselves its EASY.
5. Might need to buy the book "*Think and Grow Rich*". Or any Motivational Books.
6. Believe we can do it, and Believe it will happen.
7. Fill out ALL our work sheets we need them for us to succeed.
8. Create a plan *(goals)* that will be short term first, then some long term bigger goals.
9. Take Baby Steps *(but don't stay in diapers forever)*
10. Look at our Net Worth and make a plan to Increase it.
11. Work Smart!
12. Remember our relationship with God. REST in Him. And Time with Family.

Look what we just did. We made some obtainable Goals! By the way you need to look at and read out loud every day all your short term and long term goals.

In the beginning I really believed that goals were not necessary and I refused to write them down. I thought I would just keep them up in my head. It was amazing thought what happened the moment I wrote them down and read them every day. And then actually put them into Action!

Now we move onto one of the most important Relationships we will ever have: Family!

How sad it is that so many folks get so caught up in living in the world they tend to neglect their family. Then when they come to the end of their days it's all they desire to just have a little more time with their loved ones. **Time is not on our side**. We must make every moment count with our loved ones. Create memories that will last generations.

Folks I Love These 2 Lines from a country song by Kenny Chesney; and it is so True!

A Hundred Years Goes By Faster Than You Think So <u>Don't</u> _____!

Take Every Breath God Gives You For What Its Worth <u>Don't</u> _____!

Copyright R.E.E.D. 2008

Section 8

Family Influence

Section 8 and I don't mean Government housing; however some of you have 30 year old kids still living at home.

I'm talking about an inheritance and not just a financial one. I'm talking about leaving your family and kids some values. Training them in the way they should go.

Proverbs 22:6

> 6 Train a child in the way he should go,
>   and when he is old he will not turn from it

We parents are put in charge by God to train our kids to be Faithful Stewards.

We need to communicate with our kids in what they should do with money and what God wants them to know about money. **We need to show them and lead them by example**. We need to be a good example for our children on how we make money, spend money, and our overall attitude towards having it in abundance or having very little of it. We need to get them trained on how to be good and faithful stewards.

Once your kids start receiving money (allowances, for work / chores) we need to help them create a budget. We also need to teach them on how to Tithe, how to also invest and save. When we do this and do it regularly we are training them in the way they should go.

We need to create a budget that is just for them and done weekly. Once the monies are disbursed to the allocated goals, let them handle their money and see what happens by the end of the week. This is a great exercise and teaching opportunity. Most kids will have spent all their money before the week is out. By the way you will be tempted to help them out but DON'T!

They need to learn that being a faithful steward is very important. They need to give first to God, and with the right attitude. Keep in mind God wants us to be cheerful givers.

Corinthians 9:7

> 7 Each man should give what he has decided in his heart to give, not reluctantly or under compulsion, for God loves a cheerful giver.

Copyright R.E.E.D. 2008

We also need to teach our children how to handle what has been left as an inheritance.

So many times these days I see a TV show where some rich kid whose grandfather made millions from nothing, goes and leaves it to their grandkids who have never worked a day in their life. You see them on these shows because these shows like to show people who act like fools. Well that is what happens when a child has not been trained in the way to go. When they do not know what work really is, or that it is good to work. They seem to think they will always have money coming in. No one ever even taught them how to invest.

I like these 2 scriptures a lot.

1 Corinthians 4:2

2 Now it is required that those who have been given a trust must prove faithful.

Luke 16:1-3

1 Jesus told his disciples: "There was a rich man whose manager was accused of wasting his possessions. 2 So he called him in and asked him, 'What is this I hear about you? Give an account of your management, because you cannot be manager any longer.'"

Let me tell you the stories I have heard of people who have been left inheritances from family members and they were not qualified to handle these tasks. They lose their houses and personal items all the time in probate situations. Usually the heirs did not take care of the situations in time or at all. They have no clue what to do.

I even wrote a real estate book on how to buy these properties way below value. I felt at least we had a chance to help them before they lost it to the state or foreclosure. Other scenarios such as foreclosures are a sign that many folks are not trained on how to handle finances. And are not faithful stewards.

I'm sure we have all heard about those lottery winners who end up broke again in just a few years.

So let's train our kids and our family.

Copyright R.E.E.D. 2008

Let's start with training them what we have learned so far. But break it down to their level of understanding.

1. Income = Allowances for whatever work they are doing. From cleaning their rooms to shredding papers in your office to mowing the lawns, they need to learn how to work.
2. Tithing = Give back 1st to God what God has so lovingly given to you. Teach them that by given with the right attitude and right heart. They actually can be rewarded more.

Proverbs 11:25

25 A generous man will prosper;
he who refreshes others will himself be refreshed

Matthew 6:20-21

20 But store up for yourselves treasures in heaven, where moth and rust do not destroy, and where thieves do not break in and steal. 21For where your treasure is, there your heart will be also.

Malachi 3:10

10 Bring the whole tithe into the storehouse, that there may be food in my house. _____ in this," says the LORD Almighty, "and see if I will not throw open the floodgates of heaven and pour out so much blessing that **you will not have room enough for it.**

3. Savings = Open a savings account, CD, Or a College directed, IRA teach them it is for the future and their Children's children.
4. Investing = Let them invest in something you invest in: stocks, bonds, Real estate.
5. Goals = Their Future: help them plan there goals for the future i.e. college, trade school whatever they may have an interest in, and base it on their gifts and talents.
6. The Balance (what's left over) = Whatever is left over let them handle it and see what they do. Then re evaluate after a week and use the lesson to teach them some experiences you yourself have gained from mis-using money.

Remember they are your children but they are also God's. If you have older children find out where they are with God, what are their beliefs. This is a time to have communications. And a time to build relationships. Older children should share in the family budgeting. Let them give some input, this is how they learn. You are the teacher and God has entrusted these children to You!

Copyright R.E.E.D. 2008

Here are other subjects to talk to our kids about or get them involved in.

1. Let's talk about helping them to become wise consumers.

2. Needs vs. Wants.

3. Waiting on the Lord to provide.

4. Benefits of investing also benefits of compound interest

5. Involve your children in your work.

6. Earn Extra money by doing extra work.

7. Talk about regulating their TV, Video games etc…

8. Talk about discipline and the consequences of being disobedient.

9. Offer advice on how to Give, Save, and Spend

10. Have family time together to discuss tithing and giving.

Now we also have used a contract with our kids to show them what we expect from them and what they can expect from us. We actually went over it as a family and made sure we all were clear on what it meant to sign and the consequences of breaking it. I have attached the one we use on the next page.

Now remember we are not trying to be tyrants, we just want to get our kids use to what happens in the real world when they are old enough to sign contract, go to work for business and what those business expect from them. We are also showing them just how much we care and love them.

Now I know they might not see that at first depending on the age of your children, but our kids actually got dressed up in their business suits for that family meeting while my wife and I sit there in our night clothes. They also called me on my home office phone to remind me I was late for the meeting and if I was not there in 5 minutes they would need to re schedule. And I kid you not.

Anyway go over the contract on the next page and modify as needed for your kids and their ages.

Copyright R.E.E.D. 2008

Parent / Children Rules Agreement Contract

When you:

1. Do not obey your parents
2. Do not do your chores
3. Do not clean your Room
4. Do not do your homework
5. Do not pick up after yourselves
6. Talk back to your parents
7. Yell at each other in anger
8. Fight with each other
9. Lie
10. Steal

And / or any other * <u>inappropriate</u> thing, or if we have to tell you more than <u>once</u>!

*Inappropriate = Bad Attitude, No Manners, Facial Expressions of attitude. You know what is right and wrong!

You will lose 1 or more of the following:

1. MP3 Players
2. Phones
3. Video and any other games
4. TV privileges
5. Friends Staying the night
6. Pool privileges
7. Playing outside

You may also end up getting a belt used on your butt!

___

We as Parents Agree To

1. Help you to know and grow in your relationship with God
2. Feed You, Clothe You
3. Provide Shelter
4. Provide an Education
5. Pay Allowances for good, hard work
6. Help you to achieve your Goals.
7. Teach and help guide you on how to reach investment goals.
8. Encourage and Lead you to become Good Honorable Men and Women one day so you may teach your children the same one day.

By signing you agree that you understand this agreement, and agree it is fair punishment since only you can make the **choices.** We love you and we do this because we love you. Our part we do anyway because we want to, and because we are proud to call you our children.

Love
Mom & Dad

Child 1   Child 2

_____   _____

Copyright R.E.E.D. 2008

Now you may be thinking wow that's kind of tough. Really it's not. We have an understanding and they know exactly in most cases what they did wrong and we discipline them just as God disciplines us.

By the way here is a great scripture to remember.

Hebrews 12:6, 11

6 because the Lord disciplines those he loves,
and he punishes everyone he accepts as a son.

11 No discipline seems pleasant at the time, but painful. Later on, however, it produces a harvest of righteousness and peace for those who have been trained by it.

I know I don't like discipline either but I still get disciplined by God and after awhile I realized it helped me grow, and sometimes even gave me a little wisdom. But I'm still not real fond of it.

Now I remember growing up and my dad did not have a contract with me and my brother. He had made it very clear there was just only one punishment available in our house and we knew we didn't want it at all. Now days it is amazing how kids can get parents in trouble with different government agencies for having disciplined them. It also tells me those kids were not trained in the beginning the way God instructs us to in the Bible.

Colossians 3:19-21

19 Husbands, love your wives and do not be harsh with them.

20 Children, obey your parents in everything, for this pleases the Lord.

21 Fathers, do not embitter your children, or they will become discouraged

Remember this scripture it says a lot about the family, love, and the fruit of the Spirit.

Galatians 5:22-23

22 But the fruit of the Spirit is love, joy, peace, patience, kindness, goodness, faithfulness,
23 gentleness and self-control. Against such things there is no law.

Copyright R.E.E.D. 2008

Section 9

God, Church, the Marketplace / Tithe & Giving

Wow what a title! And yes we are going to cover it ALL!

God, church and the marketplace, and we seem to separate it just like that. But we need to be aware that that is not how God intends it to be. In fact one of the best books I have ever read is **Ed Silvoso's Anointed for Business**. In the book it shows how we are not to separate God, Church and business. There are a lot of scriptures in the bible that show this.

We need to make this a primary focus in our daily lives; we need to do our work unto the Lord. To use the work place to serve God. To be a witness at our jobs, and with our coworkers.

Colossians 3:23-24

23 Whatever you do, work at it with all your heart, as working for the Lord, not for men, 24 since you know that you will receive an inheritance from the Lord as a reward. It is the Lord Christ you are serving.

Today we see almost an attack on Christianity. We have had judges remove the "Ten Commandments" from government buildings. Our schools have removed prayer and God from the campus. If you speak up for what the word says you're persecuted. You are called names and ridiculed for "**not understanding**".

Amazingly the biggest attacks seem to be in the Christian community. You cannot condemn gay marriage, abortion, porn etc… and if you do you are really in for it. But yet attacks on Christianity seem to be ok!

I just do not understand why our country and Christians let it happen.

Maybe it's because we are too focused on our worldly lives and trying to get ahead and succeed. Maybe it's because we just don't know what to do or how to get things changed.

Well one reason I feel why this is happening is because we have separated work and church from God. **So many Christians are only focused on God on Sunday mornings**. We need to truly do our work as though we are working for the Lord. We need to bring Jesus into the work place with us everyday.

And if you are an employer make it **your** responsibility to give freedom to your employees to speak about God. **Also help them to become debt Free.**

In **Anointed for Business** there is a section on helping the people around you succeed as you succeed. Meaning as you move up in **economic levels** you are helping, *as Ed says*, your _____ **of** _____ move up with you. He mentions the more you help those around you **the more God will entrust to you**. In fact he says we cannot move up to far without bringing them with us.

I like this analogy

The Body of Christ grows proportionally. In the Body of Christ we are members of one another. How much God entrusts to you is determined by the position of the _____ **Christian** in your **Sphere of Influence.**

That still blows me away every time I read it. In fact you might stick this one on your bathroom mirror.

Now let's move to the Church in Ed's book page 108 – 109 you got to read this. By the way you've got to get his book.

"As long as we believe that the Church was born between four walls, we will always need four walls to have church"!

Amen!

I have been in many a church where the focus is the building, the funds, and growth. Somehow the focus has moved in many churches, **from the people to the bottom line**. So concerned with becoming a mega church or building expansions that we forgot what God is all about; **Remember Relationships?** He created us for that. We need to get the church back on track. Fact is many churches spend there time talking bad about the church down the street or a particular denomination. Seems they forgot who's church it is;

Jesus! We are his church, the Bride! He's coming back for us one day. And I wonder if we still sound like the Pharisees and the Sadducees to him.

Remember this: We need to Love and care about everyone, it's what Jesus did when he was here and we are supposed to be like him.

My friend Tim says this all the time;

Jesus always met people where they were!

Copyright R.E.E.D. 2008

Now Lets talk about Tithe & Giving

Let's start with some statistics; there are over ____ verses on prayer in the Bible. Less than ____ on faith, but more than _____ verses on money!

Money, money, money   MONEY!

Money & Processions have always competed with the Lord.

Matthew 6:24

24 "No one can serve two masters. Either he will hate the one and love the other, or he will be devoted to the one and despise the other. **You cannot serve both God and Money**.

I know this was the biggest hurdle for me in my life to get over. I remember saying I will give God what I have left over. Or God doesn't need **MY** money. After I had gone through 12 week stewardship training did I come to realize **everything I had was from God** and I was just the _____. He is the Lord and owner of it **ALL!** We need to understand this, believe this and then **live it**. _____ **is God's!**

1 Chronicles 29:11

11 Yours, O LORD, is the greatness and the power
and the glory and the majesty and the splendor,
for **everything in heaven and earth is yours**.

Psalm 24:1

1 The earth is the LORD's, and **everything in it**,
the world, and all who live in it;

Deuteronomy 10:14

14 To the LORD your God belong the heavens, even the highest heavens, the earth and **everything in it.**

Haggai 2:8

8 'The silver is mine and the gold is mine,' declares the LORD Almighty.

Copyright R.E.E.D. 2008

Try saying this when you talk about the possessions you have. It really is what worked for me, but it did take some time.

My money, My car, My house, My business, My church, My way, My etc…..

Replace it with this;

God's money, God's car, God's house, God's business, God's church, God's way (will) God's etc…

It will take some time but it is very powerful.

The training I went through talked about ____ **part and** _____ **part**. We each had a responsibility.

Mine was really simple, yet so hard sometimes for all of us, and that is to _____!

God's part is to _____.

And it means to really **rely on God, rest in Him.**

Matthew 11:28-30

28"Come to me, all you who are weary and burdened, and **I will give you rest**. 29Take my yoke upon you and learn from me, for I am gentle and humble in heart, and you will find rest for your souls. 30 **For my yoke is easy and my burden is light**."

Our part breaks down to this;

1 Corinthians 4:2

2Now it is required that those who have been given a trust must **prove faithful.**

Here is what we need to do;

1. <u>Be</u> _____
2. <u>Be</u> _____

   Hosea 4:6   6 my people are destroyed from lack of knowledge.

3. <u>Be</u> _____
4. <u>Work</u> _____
5. <u>Be</u> _____

Copyright R.E.E.D. 2008

We need to really pray about giving **our,** (*WOOPS*) _____ money back to Him in our tithe.

We talked about teaching our children how to tithe but remember they learn by example and we need to be Faithful at giving back to God what is actually his. So as you may have noticed by now I have used some scriptures more than once. They are some of my favorites and they really do provide a strong insight on some of these topics.

So here are some we used previously in Section 8 Family Influence.

Proverbs 11:25

25 A generous man will prosper;
he who refreshes others will himself be refreshed

Matthew 6:20-21

20But store up for yourselves treasures in heaven, where moth and rust do not destroy, and where thieves do not break in and steal. 21For where your treasure is, there your heart will be also.

Malachi 3:10

10 Bring the whole tithe into the storehouse, that there may be food in my house. **Test me** in this," says the LORD Almighty, "and see if I will not throw open the floodgates of heaven and pour out so much blessing that **you will not have room enough for it.**

Ok that was a lot so let's take a break!

But do not forget this. If we give sparingly we will receive sparingly!

Now find that scripture on your own.

You do know that the bible is a great book to read, it's motivational, it's a fantastic guide on life, and by the way when you read it God speaks to you. In fact you may have an _____ **God** moment.

Also the title of a great bible study book. Check it out!

Section 10

Investing & New or Improved Businesses

Now we get to some really good stuff on how to increase our Income. By now you have told yourself either I'm in or out. So let's keep you in, let me get your attention with making more money. But first let's implement some guidelines.

Philippians 4:11-12

11 I am not saying this because I am in need, for I have learned to **be content** whatever the circumstances. 12 I know what it is to be in need, and I know what it is to have plenty**. I have learned the secret of being content** in any and every situation, whether well fed or hungry, whether living in plenty or in want.

First thing to remember is if we increase our income we might face a major problem. That problem is that Wealth leads sometimes away from God!

Deuteronomy 31:20

20 When I have brought them into the land flowing with milk and honey, the land I promised on oath to their forefathers, **and when they eat their fill and thrive, they will turn to other gods and worship them, rejecting me** and breaking my covenant.

1 Timothy 6:17

17 Command those who are rich in this present world not to be arrogant **nor to put their hope in wealth, which is so uncertain, but to put their hope in God**, who richly provides us with everything for our enjoyment.

We may need to think more on the contentment side of where we are. What I mean is do not wear yourself out to get rich. Let's just work on becoming debt free, and being better stewards with what we already have. Let's pray and seek God for answers to taking on extra work or starting new business. It may not be in His Plans for us yet. Remember it has to be in God's time.

I want us to look at contentment some more before we move on to how to start a new business or increase the efficiency of the one we already have. On the next page we have a few more scriptures and then we will look at increasing our Income.

Copyright R.E.E.D. 2008

1 Timothy 6:8

8 But if we have food and clothing, **we will be content with that**.

Matthew 19:23

23 Then Jesus said to his disciples, "I tell you the truth, **it is hard for a rich man to enter the kingdom of heaven."**

Let's keep some things in perspective.

1. We need to live with an _____ perspective.
2. We need to pray about _____ decisions.
3. Remember _____ is His so seek the Lords Guidance.

1 Thessalonians 4:11-12

11 Make it your **ambition to lead a quiet life, to mind your own business and to work with your hands,** just as we told you, 12 so that your daily life may win the respect of outsiders and so that you will not be dependent on anybody.

God also gives us the ability to Prosper, to use what talents and wisdom He has given us to be used to make sound decisions as long as we are seeking Him first.

Deuteronomy 8:16-18

16 He gave you manna to eat in the desert, something your fathers had never known, to humble and to test you so that in the end it might go well with you. 17 **You may say to yourself, "My power and the strength of my hands have produced this wealth for me." 18 But remember the LORD your God, for it is he who gives you the ability to produce wealth,** and so confirms his covenant, which he swore to your forefathers, as it is today.

Copyright R.E.E.D. 2008

So how can we make some investments? We have mentioned several ways but we want to do something that we might know about. Let's look at real estate, if I want to make extra money in **real estate or start a new real estate business**. I might need some knowledge to make it work. I guess I could always take a stab at it, but what if I fail?

Well let us take a look at maybe another type of business maybe investing in stocks. Now for me that is gambling, because I really do not understand it. How about just sticking the money in a safe little ol' CD?

Well we have a lot to think about here. What's going to make the most for us with the least amount of risk? What if we move in a whole different direction and let's say we open a restaurant, or a computer program company. The key is this we have to go back to our God's Will For Us sheet in section 3. Pray about this and when we feel God is letting us move forward then remove the thought of fear and just rely on God to provide. It's His part, but your part might be to get some knowledge or training on the business you have chosen.

But first let's learn some basic about investing and getting **a good return on our investment**. In almost any business you need to look at how much **money you have to invest** including everything from training, start up, purchase, marketing, etc… To once it is up and running how much is **coming back in after all expenses.** Then you simply divide the net Profit or Cash Flow by the amount invested and it gives you actual cash on cash return.

Most investors in the marketplace are trying to get the highest return on investment they can. They want to know that when they put their money in an investment they are going to get the initial investment back along with a profit. What amazes me is folks who have a little bit of money here and there do not have it working for them at all. In fact it is not even in a bank earning at least 1% or something.

Now look carefully at this scripture.

Matthew 25:24-28

24"Then the man who had received the one talent came. 'Master,' he said, 'I knew that you are a hard man, harvesting where you have not sown and gathering where you have not scattered seed. 25 **So I was afraid and went out and hid your talent in the ground.** See, here is what belongs to you.'

26"His master replied, **'You wicked, lazy servant!** So you knew that I harvest where I have not sown and gather where I have not scattered seed? 27 **Well then, you should have put my money on deposit with the bankers, so that when I returned I would have received it back with interest.**

28" **'Take the talent from him and give it to the one who has the ten talents.**

Copyright R.E.E.D. 2008

That is a very strong scripture. Several things stand out.

1. The servant was afraid
2. He buried the money so as not to lose any
3. His master called him lazy
4. Then his master says something that has always interested me: "**you should have put my money on deposit with the bankers, so that when I returned I would have received it back with interest.**"

Even back then they wanted to earn some interest. Now I have heard a Christian author one time say that even in the bank it was considered **idle money.** That it still was not pleasing to God because it was put there out of fear. God wants his people to trust him and not be so concerned on losing the money that the fear of loss becomes there focus. Well anyway it is definitely interesting.

Well let's look at some examples of how we could increase our earning power by investing in things with _____ **interest**.

Compound interest is a way to earn more by leaving an investment in usually long term. And the interests you make gets added to the initial investment so you are earning interest on the investment & the interest you earned so far. Many of you might have an IRA, Mutual Fund something that is earning more than a simple 2% savings account.

When you put money into the right investment it can earn a lot for you. Such as in real estate you can **earn cash flow each month** off a rental property. But you are also **building equity** in the property every time your renters pay rent. They are paying down the mortgage balance for you.

Keep in mind also that the property may actually be **appreciating** which is **increasing your equity** even more. Now that is how I was able to **become debt free by using real estate as a vehicle** that could earn what some call **multiple streams of Income**. I had **rental properties**, I had properties I didn't even own but had under contract to buy. But I would sell them to other investors before I had to close for a fee. **We call that flipping or wholesaling**, and that created immediate cash for me. Then I had partners who put up the money to **buy, fix and then sell** those properties. Those created bigger hits for me.

Real Estate also provided some **tax benefits**, along with the ability at certain times to refinance rental properties and pull cash out of them. By the way it was usually **tax free cash**.

The main thing about real estate as a vehicle for me was I did not have to have any money to do it. In fact today I still almost never use any of my own money to do any deal. I have many ways to get the cash for a deal, if I even need cash.

Well let's let at those interest (money making charts)

Copyright R.E.E.D. 2008

Check out this little chart and remember the most valuable asset you have ever been given is _____! And **we cannot control time.**

Example 1

Now answer this question: Who do you think would accumulate more by age **65**? A person who started to save $1000 a year at age 21, saved for 8 years and then completely stopped?

Or a person who saved $1000 a year for 37 years who started at age 29?

Both **earn 10%** on their savings.

Is it the person who saved a total of $8000 or the one who saved $37,000? See the chart on the next page.

This is powerful.

Example 2   I also like this one, what would you rather have a penny a day that would double every day for 30 days or $1,000,000 *yeah one million dollars!*

Things that make you go Hummm!

By the way a penny that doubles every day goes something like this

Day 1 = .1   Day 2 = .2   Day 3 = .4   Day 5 = .8   Day 6 = .16
Day 7 = .32   Day 8 = .64   Day 9 = 1.28   Day 10 = 2.56   Day 11 = 5.12
Day 12 = 10.24   Day 13 = 20.48   Day 14 = 40.96   Day 15 = 81.92   Day 16 = 163.84

Now were just over half way there how does it look so far?

Day 17 = 327.68   Day 18 = 655.36   Day 19 = 1,310.72 Day 20 = 2,621.44 Day 21 = 5,242.88
Day 22 = 10,485.76   *Need more room*   Day 23 = 20,971.52   Day 24 = 41,943.04
Day 25 = 83,886.08   Day 26 = 167,772.16   Day 27 = 335,544.32

Well I think you get the point. I know it's killing you to find out what happens with only 3 days left.

Well you can work it out later we don't have time right now we need to find out what happened to the 2 folks above who are saving for retirement.

Come on let's look at the next page. It's **Example 1**

Copyright R.E.E.D. 2008

	Person A		**Person B**	
Age	Contribution	Year end Value	Contribution	Year end Value
21	$1000	1,100	$0	0
22	$1000	2,310	$0	0
23	$1000	3,641	$0	0
24	$1000	5,105	$0	0
25	$1000	6,716	$0	0
26	$1000	8,487	$0	0
27	$1000	10,436	$0	0
28	**$1000**	**12,579**	**$0**	**0**
29	$0	13,837	$1000	1,100
30	$0	15,221	$1000	2,310
31	$0	16,743	$1000	3,641
32	$0	18,417	$1000	5,105
33	$0	20,259	$1000	6,716
34	$0	22,284	$1000	8,487
35	$0	24513	$1000	10436
36	$0	26,964	$1000	12,579
37	$0	29,661	$1000	14,937
38	$0	32,627	$1000	17,531
39	$0	35,889	$1000	20,384
40	$0	39,478	$1000	23,523
41	$0	43,426	$1000	26,975
42	$0	47769	$1000	30,772
43	$0	52,546	$1000	34,950
44	$0	57,800	$1000	39,545
45	$0	63,580	$1000	44,599
46	$0	69,938	$1000	50,159
47	$0	76,932	$1000	56,275
48	$0	84,625	$1000	63,003
49	$0	93,088	$1000	70,403
50	$0	103,397	$1000	78,543
51	$0	112,636	$1000	87,497
52	$0	123,898	$1000	97,347
53	$0	136,290	$1000	108,182
54	$0	149,919	$1000	120,100
55	$0	164,911	$1000	133,210
56	$0	181,402	$1000	147,631
57	$0	199,542	$1000	163,494
58	$0	219,496	$1000	180,943
59	$0	241,446	$1000	200,138
60	$0	265,590	$1000	221,252
61	$0	292,149	$1000	244,477
62	$0	321,364	$1000	270,024
63	$0	353,501	$1000	298,127
64	$0	388,851	$1000	329,039
65	**$0**	**427,736**	**$1000**	**363,043**

Total Invested $8000 $37,000

Copyright R.E.E.D. 2008

Well what do you think? **Powerful**? I think so.

So as far as investments we need to **make our money work hard for us**. If we start a new business we might have to work hard at it but will it make us enough extra money to pay off our debt? Keep in mind we are still trying to **reduce our debt as our primary focus.** But at the same time we are looking to see if we can **increase our income** by taking on extra work, starting a side business, or making some good investments that will produce some strong returns.

Now before we go jumping into anything remember we need to **go to God and pray** to see if it's what he wants us to do. **Are the doors opening** for us to go in that direction? Do we have a **peace about it**? Or is he making us wait? Could He just be waiting for us to **step out in faith** and give it a shot? Sometimes God likes to see us take some steps of faith. If we make a wrong choice He usually can use that for his better purpose. Remember keep going over Section 3 Gods Will For Us. That has helped me make decisions many, many times.

Well were almost done. It's time to put all this together. Get a perspective of what we have learned so far. We need a lot of step by step things to happen really soon. So these last 2 sections are about getting this all implemented and in to an Action plan that will succeed.

I'm also going to go into more depth of how I used real estate to become personally debt free. At the same time I was creating some smart business debt to increase my income.

So let's get ready, we have a lot to do, and a short time to get it done!

Section 11

Putting It All Into Perspective

Ok! Now What? How do we start to **implement all we have learned** so far? There's a lot to do. And for many of us it may be overwhelming. So we need to but some things into perspective.

Main thing for you to know is that the last section is called **Action Plan**. And it is what will give us a step by step check list of things to get done. But I want to talk about the **Big** _____. What I mean is where are we going with this training. What are our goals upon completion of this training?

If we are so overwhelmed we most likely won't do anything. So let's step back and take a look at everything we've learned.

First thing is, understand you do not have **to tackle it all** at once. We do not have to go to such extremes as calculating how much mustard to use on each hamburger so we stay in budget. What we should do is look at some of the basics.

1. How much money do we make each month?
2. Are we using the money wisely?
3. Is there a way for us to increase the amount we make each month?
4. Could we take on some extra side jobs to increase the revenue?
5. Can we put some of the money into some investments that would bring in extra money?
6. What kind of investments could we put the money in to accomplish this?
7. Can we create a business that is self sufficient or requires little of our time?
8. Do we have the skills or knowledge to create and operate it successfully?
9. Would real estate be a possibility for us?
10. What kind of real estate could we do that would create income, and not take all of our TIME?

These are some **Big Picture** Questions we need to answer. If we can get this part done first then we are on our way to making extra income each month.

Then we can get to the part of **reducing our debt** and paying off the debt we currently have as fast as we can. Remember _____ and _____ are working against us in the debt part of our lives. We also want to look at **retiring** someday. Now I do not mean the retirement of sitting around the rest of our days doing nothing. I mean retiring from having to work all the time so you can get by and pay your bills.

One day our goal is to be able to **spend more** _____ serving God and doing his will. And if we are ____ _____ and have extra income coming in we can do that. Now the way I was able to do this was through real estate investing. I started out investing while I was still employed in the electronics business. I did not have any extra money but as we talked earlier

I had gone through some real estate training courses that showed me several ways to make money with no money. Thanks to those courses I had several ways to **generate extra income**. The key was to take **that income and re invest to make more income**. However in the beginning that is not what Rachell and I did. **Oh no we became connoisseurs in the art of spending money.**

We literally bought everything in site and took every vacation imaginable. Then we would come back and realize we were still dead broke. Finally we decided to look at investing the monies we made, and agreeing to only blow 10% of all the profit. Now I do not encourage this theory but for us it was better than blowing 100%.

Finally as we bought more rental properties, our cash flow increased, and of course we continued to wholesale and rehab properties for immediate cash. **We would re invest the cash and do it all over again.**

Now the next important step was to **seek the counsel** of our CPA. He showed us how to set up an **entity** and create different retirement perks through those companies and use a lot of government programs and rules to keep our taxes low while adding to our _____ **fund**. To this day we have realized that if we do not put money back for our future now, we may face some really hard times when we get older. We also want to be able to leave our **children an inheritance**. Not only for them, but for their children, too. In doing so I noticed that some of what we are leaving them has not even reached it's peak and may not for years to come. What I'm talking about is the ability **for real estate to go up in** _____ **over** _____.

Think back 30 years in time and at the prices of real estate back then. It was really cheap, and keep in mind how much they went up based on **different markets**; Areas like California, Washington, New York, and Florida have all gone up tremendously over the years.

Now don't get me wrong; there are a lot of ways to make money out there. I just want to show you how I did it. And hopefully encourage you to believe that whatever you decide to do, you can make it happen **if you work hard at it**. And that you do not have to be some kind of honor graduate, or rocket scientist to do it. I am living proof of that, I was very consistent in school all 12 grades, and some college. **I consistently did very badly!**

So don't do what a lot of folks do and that is to try and talk them out of being successful. Convincing themselves they can never do it because they never have done well in school. Or they feel they just are not that smart.

Remember **God created you** to do great things. **You just have to have Faith**! By the way part of the **big picture** is that **real estate** was one of the main things that were *promised, given to, or fought for through out the Bible*. Check out the scriptures on the next page.

Copyright R.E.E.D. 2008

Genesis 12:7
The LORD appeared to Abram and said, "To your offspring I will give this **land**."

Genesis 26:4
I will make your descendants as numerous as the stars in the sky and will give them all these **land**s, and through your offspring all nations on earth will be blessed

Joshua 23:4
Remember how I have allotted as an **inheritance** for your tribes all the **land** of the nations that remain

Job 22:8
though you were a powerful man, owning **land**— an honored man, living on it.

Psalm 37:11
But the meek will inherit the **land** and enjoy great peace.

Psalm 37:29
the righteous will inherit the **land** and dwell in it forever.

It seems in the Old Testament that a lot of what was going on happen to involve land. So as we look at putting all this training into perspective keep in mind that real estate has a lot of value and when you couple the necessities of life to it, you have a **real strong investment**.

In closing on the Big Picture let's not forget we may not know our future but we should definitely plan for it. Let us use the wisdom and knowledge that the Lord has blessed us with to make smart decisions.

As we move on to our last Section we need to keep in our **mind set** that **we are 3%**. We need to keep the **big picture at the top of our mind set**. We want to be prepared in our Golden Years. I could not imagine ever going to a nursing home. I want to prepare my family financially to take care of me, if needed right at home. One thing we must have as part of the big picture is _____ _____. We really have not talked about it but we do need it. We must have enough there to cover our family, and pay for all their needs. We want to have enough to take care of funeral arrangements and cover all the cost related to it. Don't forget we need a _____. What a mess we can create by not having a will. Remember I have bought real estate way below value because someone thought they would get to it later, well later came before they were ready!

Lastly if you own real estate put them in a _____ or have your _____ **IRA** own them, You now can **by pass some probate**, pass the beneficiary to your kids, and oh yeah **not pay taxes** on any of the profit!   *Oh how we need the Big Picture Stuff!*

Copyright R.E.E.D. 2008

Section 12

Action Plan

Yeah one last step! With only 30 things to do!

Ok it's time to roll all this up into one giant to do list. So here we go:

1. **Seek a regular time daily to spend with God.**

2. **Read His word, and be still and listen.**

3. Then approach God in **prayer**, real prayer time you set aside that you give Praise to Him for who He is. The give thanks for all he has done. Remember to confess our wrongs. Make sure you pray for other's (intercessor prayer) and lastly present God with your request. Keep in mind if you believe and it is His will then it is done in His time!

4. After praying we need to fill out our **Talents & Gift** sheet. Remember it is based on what we think they are right now.

5. Then let's look at **WORK**, do we need to do extra work to increase our Income. Do we feel God wants us to take this on? Our goal is to earn more to reduce personal debt.

6. Let's now fill out the **Fact sheet**. List the skill we now we have right now. List some we would like to learn.

7. What kind of business would we like to be in? Do you think God has given you the gifts to do it? May need more prayer.

8. Remember **Supply and demand**, without this we could wind up in more trouble.

Copyright R.E.E.D. 2008

9. Will we need to **get trained** to do this new business?

10. Can we approach it with a **3% attitude**, be a **Problem Solver**?

11. Most of all lets do it with **Excellence and for the Lord**!

12. Do we have a team to help us, or a Mentor who has been there, done that?

13. Section 3 **"Gods Will for Us"**. Go back over this at home in a very quiet place. Maybe get up one morning really early and just read God's word and then go through the worksheet, and see where God leads you. Read all the scriptures in this section. Keep in mind as you go through it is it Biblical, Do you have a Peace about it, and is the opportunity there?

14. Section 4 You have to fill out the **Personal Financial Statements** and this will take a little time but you must do it. Gather all the info so you can start to get a picture of where you are.

15. Next fill out the **Monthly Budget**, now this will probably take a lot of time. Again it has to be done if we truly want to become debt free. As you fill it out think about some alternatives to getting the debt paid off. *Could you take the smallest credit card balance and double up on the payment adding principal only payments to it?* Once paid off the monthly payment just got dropped a little, and now you can double up on another one and repeat the process.

16. **Financial Goals** 2 pages in length and well worth spending some major time analyzing it. Start with the tithe; if we are not giving in faith, sincerity, or with a **cheerful heart**, it matters not. God doesn't need your money, He wants to see you give because of the love you have for Him. Remember *Malachi 3: 8-10 read it regularly*.

17. Then set the **Debt Goals**, create some obtainable goals on getting these debts paid off. Credit cards only are the focus for these page you will do the other debts later.

18. Set some **Investment Goals** you need to start investing you money to make a profit. We are managers of what God has given you, manage it well.

19. If you have kids or grandkids start an **Education Goal**. List on that page the goals for education. Maybe it's training for you in your new or current business.

20. Start a **Savings Goal**; don't count on the government to take care of you. Social Security probably won't be around and from what I see now it's not enough to pay your bills.

21. **Starting a Business** is this a goal for you? Have you already started one? Do you have goals to reach? Do you have a Business Plan with timelines?

22. Now this one even I can't stand to do, fill out the **Debt Reduction List**. Get all the major and minor debts. on this list and take a long hard look at it. Because the next form is how we get it paid off. Get creative too on how to make extra principal payments to reduce the balances and pay them off early.

23. The **Debt Schedule** we have to keep at this monthly. Be strong no exceptions make the payments. Keep to the plan. Remember the Interest is robbing you of your funds!

24. **Budget Goals Sheet**, this is where I spent a lot of time when we were in the process of reducing our personal debt. How could I cut some things and then take the extra money and actually eliminate some debt. Her are some examples: Cable bill do you need all the movie channels? And belong to the DVD club of the month and still go out to the movies? Come on pick one as a treat when you hit some of your goals. Make sure to also Give FIRST (Tithe) then pay with whatever is left. Be faithful and God will be faithful.

Copyright R.E.E.D. 2008

25. **Work,** Work hard, Work with Excellence. Work to increase your Net Worth. But also **REST** God commands it. Work provides extra income; extra income can be invested to make more income. Then you can actually begin to eliminate debt.

26. **Family Influence**, we need to spend time with our loved ones, we need to train our children in the way they should go. We need to understand them and their needs, their personalities. We also can fill out the **Parent Children Rules Agreement**. Be clear of what you expect from your children and lift them up with praise, for one day you will be depending on them. Raise them to be Honorable, have Integrity, and good Character. Most of all Godly children who one day will teach their children what they have learned from You!

27. **God, Church, the Marketplace / Tithe & Giving** Again WOW! Here let's remember that we are witness to the world. When we are at work, with our kids, or just out in the marketplace, do we represent Christ with how we act and what we do?

What if you're at dinner and the food comes out cold, or not the right order, how do you respond?

What if after you eat and the bill comes, and you notice you were not charged some items, what will you do?

Something to think about? You need to do what is right all the time.

And when it comes to giving the tithe just do it, but do pray about the amount and to where. I really believe God wants us to pray with our spouse and family on where His money should go. Not all of it has to go to the church only. Maybe the homeless need some, how about a brother in need. *This scripture has always stood out to me*.

Proverbs 3:27-28

27 **Do not withhold good** from those who deserve it,
   when it is in your power to act.

28 Do not say to your neighbor,
   "Come back later; **I'll give it tomorrow**"—
   when you now have it with you.

We also need to become **content** with what God has already provided for us.

Remember also your Sphere of Influence. Helping those you know is a way to serve God.

28. **Investing & New or Improved Businesses** this is really important look back at the 2 examples of **compounding Interest**. Income is where I wanted to go with this training; how to make more income so we could pay off Debt faster. A lot of stewardship trainings focus on just cutting back on everything so you can add extra payments to the debt. I personally feel **God wants to bless us** and He will if we manage it all correctly. If we learn to **live below our means** and yet still comfortably. Don't go crazy spending everything you get. **Credit cards are dangerous** when not used as a proper tool for **leveraging Money**. I think for a **month or 3** try buying everything, I mean everything with cash. I think we all would spend less because **CASH is real** and Plastic is a false sense of what you actually have. What I mean is **you spend cash, and it hurts**. Plastic doesn't bother us it not real to us; Remember:

God gives us the ability to create Wealth!

I always teach in my real estate classes how to <u>Buy and Sell to create</u> _____ and how to <u>Buy & Hold to create</u> _____.

29. Now put all we have learned into **Perspective.** What can we do now, what can we do next week. Have I written down my personal goals? How about some business goals? Have I filled my mind lately with positive things? If I am a real estate Investor have I made any offers? Looked at any properties? Am I still sitting around craving Baby food? Or am I really ready to make a change?

30. **What do I do Next?** Well try starting with the **29** things we just went through. The choice to do something is **yours!**

$$ Be Prepared To Do Something Extraordinary $$
All It Takes Is Your Mind!

Romans 12:2
Do Not Conform Any Longer To The Pattern Of This World,
But Be Transformed By The Renewing Of Your Mind.

Copyright R.E.E.D. 2008

Now we are done, **yet** there is more! Let me go in detail how I became debt free by using real estate as the vehicle to do it. I want you to know right now if you have no interest in real estate you are done. Now go out and be a Faithful Steward.

And remember this scripture for as long as you are on this planet, this is going to happen someday.

Romans 14:11-13

11It is written:
 "'As surely as I live,' says the Lord,
 'every knee will bow before me;
 every tongue will confess to God.' "12So then, **each of us will give an account of himself to God.**

I hope and pray these are the answer & gifts you receive.

Matthew 25:23
"His master replied, '**Well done**, good and faithful servant!'

Revelation 22:12
"Behold, I am coming soon! My **reward** is with me, and I will give to everyone **according to what he has done.**"

God Bless You and may you reach all your Goals in Life!

Copyright R.E.E.D. 2008

NOTES

Real Estate Investing

Creative Financing

Copyright R.E.E.D. 2008

NOTES

Real Estate Investing

Wholesale

Copyright R.E.E.D. 2008

NOTES

Real Estate Investing

Probate

NOTES

Real Estate Investing

Panama

Copyright R.E.E.D. 2008

NOTES

Real Estate Investing

Costa Rica FAM Trip

Copyright R.E.E.D. 2008

About Your Instructor

Jimmy Reed has an extensive background in the field of Real Estate Investing having bought, sold and managed over 300 units all by the age of thirty. Jimmy began his investment career in the late 1980's while still working full time in electronics. Having developed a solid understanding of real estate investing, Jimmy went on to specialize in the areas of Wholesaling and cash flow Rentals.

After several years of success in the business and teaching 1 day trainings in the Dallas / Fort Worth area, a National Real Estate Consultant approached Jimmy to be involved with one of the countries top training organizations. So in May of 1997, he began teaching Wholesaling for that training company and later helped developed their one on one Mentoring program. These "training's" put Jimmy in some of the hottest markets in the country such as Hawaii, New York, Cozumel, Mexico, Panama and even Costa Rica.

Currently, Jimmy is the founder of Real Estate Equity Development, Reed Investment Property's, and Co-founder of Kingdom R.E.S.T. Companies which specialize in the buying and selling of wholesale real estate, and providing reality based information for others who want to learn about the exciting opportunities in real estate, and how to create residual income through rental properties. Along with creating the "Fast Track to Wholesaling" Training Camp he is also co author of "The Hidden Treasures and Profits of Probate" book. And the co founder of www.REIO-FW.com real estate club located in Fort Worth, TX. When he is not busy buying property or conducting real estate training, Jimmy enjoys spending time with his lovely wife and their two children. He also is an active scuba diver, and has been involved in teaching financial training courses for church.

www.JimmyReed.net

Copyright R.E.E.D. 2008